Universal Ministries Presents

"As the DEER PANTS STREAMS of WATER"

BOOK OF PRAYER & MEDITATIONS
written by *Michelle Addison Jones*

"I, therefore, contend that prayer is the bending of the will to incline one's ear to the heartbeat of God"

To order additional copies of this book, contact:
Xlibris Corporation
1-888-795-4274
www.Xlibris.com
Orders@Xlibris.com

Dedication

In memory of my beloved dad, Leonard Harry Addison, I dedicate this work to the Addison family (Narvis, Dowayne, Leonard Jr., Clifton, and Dorothy Addison—Mom), my husband, David Christopher Jones, to those who suffer loss at any level, and to every minister called by God into sacred duty.

Special thanks to the following for their unwavering moral, emotional, spiritual guidance:

Dr. Harold A. Carter & Dr. Harold A. Carter, Jr., Pastor of New Shiloh Baptist Church, Baltimore, Maryland.

Special thanks to the following for their support during the darkest season in my life:

David Christopher Jones, Husband and Friend

The Congregation of New Shiloh Baptist Church, Baltimore, Maryland

Reverend Peggy Annette Coleman – New Shiloh Baptist Church, Baltimore, Maryland

Reverend Raiza Rahim - New Shiloh Baptist Church, Baltimore, Maryland.

Above all, utmost appreciation to the Spirit of God for his divine intervention in this work.

Contents

Forward

How important is prayer to the life of a born again Christian? I would suggest that it is impossible to live a victorious life without prayer. How important is prayer to the life of a child of God? Given that prayer is communication with God, I would suggest that it is impossible to have an intimate relationship with God without prayer. How important is prayer to the life of one who professes to be a believer? Since the prayer of the righteous achieves much, I would suggest that there would be a limit to what a believer will overcome without prayer. Yet, despite its importance, many Christians are not as enthusiastic about prayer as they ought to be.

If you doubt this assertion, then let me ask you this, which event is likely to draw the larger crowd, a prayer meeting or a concert? I think you know the answer. Yet, as entertaining as the concert may be (and they do have their place in our lives), it is prayer that will do the most for us. Sadly, many of us make time for so many other activities, while prayer is often relegated to a bedtime activity; but how wonderful it would be if we were enthused to earnestly seek after God. How marvelous it would be if we hungered for the presence of God. With that in mind, I believe that reading this book will encourage you to develop a passion for prayer.

This work is a clarion call to the believer to pursue God through prayer. The book is not really a "how to" instruction manual; it is more of an ode to joys of prayer. It speaks to the comfort and reassurance we receive from being in the presence of the Lord. The inspiration derived from meditation. Minister Michelle Jones effectively communicates how powerfully therapeutic it can be to interact with God in prayer. She provides vivid accounts of her personal encounters with God that allows you to visualize the power of God in action. Since God is no respecter of persons, what we see Him do for the writer, He can and will do for us.

Minister Jones loves God and wants to help you ignite your passion for God. Let the writer lead you through the meditations. Let the writer lead you to a deeper appreciation for the greatness of God. Allow the writer to guide you to the throne room, via the scripted prayers. Once you are there, and you truly interact with God, the experience will leave you wanting more. So, be ready to be inspired. Be ready to develop that passion for God.

May God bless you, richly.
Bishop Courtney Henry

Acknowledgments

Sincere gratitude is hereby extended to the following persons, all of whom are people of honor, great integrity, genuine love for God and people, and exceptional biblical and theological insight:

The prestigious Bishop Courtney Henry, Pastor of Bibleway Truth Temple, Blackwood, New Jersey.

Eileen Eppig, SSND, Ph.D., Associate Professor of Religious Studies, College of Notre Dame of Maryland.

The prestigious Doctor David Heard, Pastor of Passtown Baptist Church, Coatesville, Pennsylvania. Reverend and Mrs. Heard are very dear friends who agreed to write a review for this book.

The prestigious Doctor Henry T. Baines, President of the Ministers & Evangelist Council at New Shiloh Baptist Church, Baltimore Maryland.

The prestigious Reverend and Mrs. William R. Brewer, Minister - New Shiloh Baptist Church, Baltimore, Maryland.

PSALMS 42 (NIV)

*As the deer pants for steams of water, so my soul pants for you, O
God.*

*My soul thirsts for God, for the living God.
When can I go and meet with God?*

*My tears have been my food day and night, while men say to me all
day long, "Where is your God?"*

*These things I remember as I pour out my soul: how I used to go
with the multitude, leading the procession to the house of God, with
shouts of joy and thanksgiving among the festive throng.*

*Why are you downcast, O my soul? Why so disturbed within me?
Put your hope in God, for I
will yet praise him, my Savior and my God.
My soul is downcast within me; therefore I
will remember you from the land of the Jordan,
the heights of Hermon—from Mount Mizar.*

*Deep calls to deep in the roar of your waterfalls; all your waves and
breakers have swept over me.
By day the LORD directs his love, at night his song is with me—a
prayer to the God of my life.*

*I say to God my Rock, "Why have you forgotten me? Why must I
go about mourning,
oppressed by the enemy?"*

*My bones suffer mortal agony as my
foes taunt me, saying to me all day long,
"Where is your God?"*

*Why are you downcast, O my soul?
Why so disturbed within me?
Put your hope in God, for I will yet
praise him, my Savior and my God.*

Introduction

Alzheimer's is a progressive disorder that affects the short-term memory and, ultimately, one or more other abilities, such as speech, mobility, judgment, and the ability to interact within your environment. Dad had reached the critical stages of Alzheimer's on March 31, 2009, and a decision was made by the family, at the recommendation of Dad's physicians, to move him to the hospice ward of Stella Maris. We were well aware that the inevitable would be days, if not moments, away and wanted Dad to be as comfortable as possible. The family gathered (grandchildren, great-grandchildren, sisters, brothers, etc.) daily in Dad's suite, as if to proclaim his crossing over to be a greatly celebrated event. Indeed, it was truly a moment to be remembered, though bittersweet . . .

On April 8, 2009, at 5:45 a.m., after struggling for approximately six to eight months with complications from Alzheimer's, I witnessed Dad exhale for the last time.

Dad did not hold a special position of authority during his service in the United States Army (WWII), nor did he achieve any special degrees for higher learning or was the author of any great books; however, he was a man of honor, and his claim to fame was that he understood something about self-sacrificial love. He received his "call" to the ministry of fatherhood at a very early age. Sacrificing his youth in exchange for the heavy responsibility of raising his sisters and providing for his dear mother was just preparation for his place in future years ahead. He grew in wisdom and become the best dad and father any child would want to have.

Thus, Dad's life story, lived out in full view for all to witness, was indeed better than any good novel that could ever have been written, or any degree ever achieved.

Dad's going-home service was a great celebration and a triumph for my family as my siblings stood before God, family, friends, and acquaintances to give tribute to his memory. Many, who knew Dad in one aspect or the other, came to pay their regards. There were a great number of men that Dad had influenced who were in attendance at the home-going service, and each of them had a story to tell of their encounter with the wisdom that flowed so easily from the heart of my dad. A few of them volunteered to be the pallbearers, stating that it would be a great honor to carry Dad's coffin. In many instances, Dad was the only father figure that they were acquainted with during their lifetime. Was Dad perfect? Of course not, which is the reason he was so special. He never tried to hide his shortcomings; rather, he was very transparent, which is the reason why the youth listened to his words of wisdom. Dad had a way of ministering to the youth, especially his own children, but we thought they were lectures at the time and could not grasp the immensity of his words until adulthood. The wisdom that God poured into his heart was profound and life-giving. His legacy will live forever through the lives of his family and every man that he influenced.

"Hope thou in God; for I shall yet praise him, who is the health of my countenance, and my God." (Psalm 42)

When Dad was first diagnosed with dementia, we were all in denial. However, as time passed and the disease progressed, we began to see the evidence and gradually began to understand the reality of the disease and the impact it would have on our family. There is no doubt that we were all "changed" by this experience. The most beautiful memory of this experience is how God used the "gifts" and special talents of each sibling to play an important role in the process of Dad's crossing over.

I can personally attest to God's amazing grace. At the moment of Dad's passing, though weak in body, shocked and grief stricken in spirit, I suddenly encountered an inner strength that was beyond the natural capacity to attain; such strength was as mysterious as is God. It seemed that my spirit had been transported into a state of total peace and tranquility—that secret place where the eternal God IS. A place of abiding rest, and complete trust and confidence in the ability of the Holy Spirit to comfort, lead, and guide in the way I should go. I knew then and even more profoundly now that I had reached a place of total weakness, thus I cannot possibly boast in myself; rather, I boast in the Lord—whose presence is indeed a present help in the time of need (Psalm 46:1).

Quickened in spirit, strengthened in faith, infused with supernatural power and the ability to stand, not even wholly cognizant of the place where I stood then but filled with a new power and vigor for God's will above my own, I was able to face death with a song in my heart and proceed with the role that was required of me to assist with the process of Dad's crossing over. Who would have imagined that I, of all my siblings, would dare to greet death with a new song in my heart? I say to you, "Death! Where is your sting? Grave! Where is your hold?" The sweet presence of the Holy Spirit carried me through the darkest moment of my life. And his abiding presence reassured me that Daddy had been ushered into that sacred place of being one with God in spirit and in essence.

My eldest brother (Leonard Addison Jr.) contends that grief is a mystery and ponders who can possibly lay hold of the claim to understand it. I agree with his sentiments. Grief is indeed a mystery and there is no easy way around it. In some mysterious way, grief is intricately woven into the fabric of life, and to try to avoid it is literally impossible. And though try as we may, busing ourselves about, nonetheless, grief will remain until we have determined in our hearts and minds that we shall face it head on and strive to live through it by the grace of the Almighty God, one day at a time.

Thus, the inspiration for developing this book was birthed out of an extraordinary journey encountered during the passing of my dear dad, Leonard Harry Addison, and God's abiding presence, which sheltered me as I walked through the valley of shadows, without whose help I never would have made it otherwise. As a result of this bitter/sweet encounter, what developed was a passion to seek the face of God and to communicate with Him on a deeper level. Little had I realized that while I was seeking after God, He was patiently waiting to draw me into a dimension of intercessory prayer that would transform my perspective about life and death, and would ultimately lead my spirit into heights of fellowship and glorious worship that I had never known was attainable in third-dimensional thought!

Thus, the mysterious wonders of God's amazing grace shifted my attention from personal sorrow to accepting the call to pray on behalf of families everywhere with special emphasis on the Ekklesia (Body of Christ) and its ministers, who, despite the vicissitudes of life, continue in their pursuit to place God's will above their own.

I dedicate this work to the precious memory of my beloved dad, to the Addison family (Narvis, Dowayne, Leonard Jr., Clifton, and Dorothy Addison—Mom), to my husband, David Christopher Jones, and to every minister called by God into sacred duty.

It is my earnest prayer before God, our most sovereign savior, that you, my dear brethren, would experience, by the full measure of his grace, total awareness of God's divine presence, providential order, and purpose as you embark on your journey into deeper dimensions of worship, prayer, and praise to the only wise God and Father of the Lord Jesus Christ.

Morning Glory

*Even when I walk
through the darkest valley,
I will not be afraid,
for you are close beside me.
Your rod and your staff
protect and comfort me.
(Psalm 23:4)*

VOLUME 1

The body is a unit, though it is made up of many parts; and though all its parts are many, they form one body. (1 Corinthians 12:12)

The Purity of Oneness

How good and pleasant it is when brothers live together in unity! It is like precious oil poured on the head, running down on the beard, running down on Aaron's beard, down upon the collar of his robes. (Psalm 133:1–2)

A Thought to Ponder

The month of March 2010 proved to be very hard for me to bear. It was just last year when Dad slowly succumbed to that state of being that is often referred to as death. But I contend and am therefore convinced by the mercies of God that "death" is indeed that eternal rest in God's presence to which we long for, reach for, and desire wholeheartedly to attain; and yet we fear the inevitable. Until that blessed day, by God's divine providence and order, we too are made to succumb and to welcome it with an opened heart.

With Dad's passing so fresh in memory, I sought with haste a place of refuge to lay my burdens down where I would not be judged by my present state of weakness. Suddenly, I found my feet planted upon the steps of an old familiar place, the Catholic church. There she stood, waiting, almost beckoning me to enter. How could I possibly resist? With pride completely obliterated by sorrow's valley and no defense to cling to, I entered her doors with a contrite heart filled with humility. Upon reaching the foyer, I heard voices from the direction of a chamber where a few of the elders engaged in symphonic prayer. It was the most beautiful sound I had ever heard! I could only imagine how pleasant it must have sound to God.

As I approached the door leading to the chamber of prayer, I witnessed a beam of brilliant light emanating through the cracks in the door. Would I dare to enter the chamber and risk interrupting the rhythmic pattern of corporate prayer? Compelled by the Holy Spirit, I continued on until my hand was upon the doorknob, turning it ever so gently until the door opened and, with entrance, revealed a wonderful presence that was so holy I could not speak. It was in that place where I laid my burdens down and the pain of loneliness and sorrow began to slowly dissipate into nothingness. There they were, all in one place of being, filled with great humility and a deep, abiding love for one another, the object of their affection and the focus of their supplications—indeed, this was true corporate prayer practiced and perfected!

There were four elders engaged in corporate prayer; of the four, two of them I recognized as Mom and her sister, Aunt Mable. Without missing a beat, they turned in unison, bowing their heads in acknowledgement of my presence with a welcoming spirit so full of love and acceptance, but never once losing the rhythm of their connectedness. Totally weak in the knees, I fell back lightly onto a crackly old wooden chair and wept profusely! I felt a sense of pouring outward all the signs of grief along with the pain of loneliness; in exchange, God filled my cup with unconditional love! I was literally overwhelmed by a great sense of satisfaction and felt that I had been enveloped by the loving presence of the Holy Spirit! Truly, I could even sense the presence of Dad's spirit, which was sweet and comforting.

Prayer

Gracious Father, King of Glory, thank you for your Ekklesia, Body of Christ—one church, one faith, one baptism, and one savior, the Lord Jesus Christ; for allowing me to lay my burdens down and to be renewed, replenished, and restored in the newly discovered freedom found in my blessed Savior. You cleansed my thoughts with your presence and filled me with a new vigor, strength, and brotherly love. O', God! You are! You are!

Sweet Holy Spirit

There's a sweet, sweet Spirit in this place,
And I know that it's the Spirit of the Lord;
There are sweet expressions on each face,
And I know that it's the presence of the
Lord.

Sweet holy Spirit,
Sweet heavenly Dove;
Stay right here with us,
Filling us with your love;

And for these blessings,
We lift our hearts in praise;
Without a doubt we'll know
That we have been revived,
When we shall leave this place.

by Doris Mae Akers

You will keep in perfect peace him whose mind is steadfast, because he trusts in you. (ISAIAH 26:3)

In Holy Union

I in them and you in me. May they be brought to complete unity to let the world know that you sent me and have loved them even as you have loved me. (John 17:23)

Gracious Lover, Supreme Sovereign, thank you for the "so love" of the Father; for the self-sacrificial yes of the Son and for the indwelling of the Holy Spirit; for that perfect union demonstrated between the Father, Son, and Holy Spirit—all one in being but three distinctive personalities, moving in syncopated rhythm with the other.

Lord Jesus, Wonderful Savior, Mighty God, we lift up marriages everywhere this morning. Help us all to understand the meaning of the phrase "The two shall become one." The kind of oneness that does not overshadow the uniqueness of the other; rather, that perfect oneness that is self-giving, self-emptying, self-sacrificial in order to bring the other to their fullest potential of being in you. This is the oneness that we hope for, reach for, and strive to attain with a whole heart, for this perfect place of being one with another.

Sweet Holy Spirit, lead and guide couples everywhere as they journey into the depth of the Father's "so love." Thank you for restoring order; for the healing of old wounds; for the miracle of touching and agreeing in the name of Jesus; for granting to us all emotional and mental stability; a willingness to demonstrate patience, kindness, and gentleness toward our spouses; for the conviction of sin and the assurance that we are forgiven.

We pray this prayer to a great god, who is well able to perform, and seal it in the prevailing name of the Lord Jesus Christ. Amen.

I beseech you that there be no divisions among you, but that ye be perfectly joined together.

(1 CORINTHIANS 1: 10)

Unity's Petition

Do not be anxious about anything, but in everything by prayer and supplication with thanksgiving let your request be made known to God. (Philippians 4:6)

Holy Sovereign—Creator, Ruler, and Sustainer of all Life, thank you for watching over us throughout the night with all diligence; for dispatching your angelic host to keep us safe as we lie in that vulnerable state of unconsciousness; for calling us to this glorious day to drink of your fount. You have already supplied our every need and have even commended your love toward us. What more is there to ask of our Great God whose name is Excellent!

Sweet Holy Spirit, All-Consuming Fire, fill us with your divine love to the overflow; help us to celebrate diversity; to be synchronized with your rhythmic patterns of movement; to have eyes to see your divine movement and be grateful; to have a heart to receive self-sacrificial love without complaint, argument, malice, bitterness, and confusion but with a joyful heart filled with adoration, praise, and thanksgiving to God! Break pride into pieces; utterly destroy the spirit of combativeness, envy, and jealousy. We ask these things of a great god, whose name is Mighty God!

Supreme Lover and Savior to the uttermost, grant us revelation of your love divine, the unity of the Trinity, Christ and the cross, self-sacrificial love.

Father, you do all things well; grant us clarity in thought, innovation, and creative power to give of ourselves freely, lovingly, and wholly, without hesitation, selfishness, or ulterior motive but wholly as unto you, may we give our all to the excellence of your great name, and may the Light of Jesus shine brightly in us on this blessed day that you have made.

We ask these things of a great god, who is well-able to perform, in the name of the Lord Jesus Christ. Amen.

" . . . and pray on my behalf, that utterance may be given to me in the opening of my mouth, to make known with boldness the mystery of the gospel.
(EPHESIANS 6:19)

Sunday's Plea

He must increase, but I must decrease. (John 3:30)

O', God of Grace, I give you thanks for this day that you have made; for the fellowship of the saints and for the preaching of your blessed Word! I pray that the purity of your Word will sanctify every minister who will stand before the congregation of your people! Let your creative Word run swiftly to divide asunder the soul from the spirit, discerning the thoughts and intents of the heart break down barriers of misconceptions and preconceived ideas, cross boundaries of ignorance, and apprehend them with your love! O', God, do this first in your ministers and let the purity of your Word move through their vessels to do what it does best: bring deliverance with a strong and mighty arm from every foul, wicked, and perverse thing that may hinder your move in the earth and in your people; heal the sick, make the blind see, the lame walk, dumb speak, deaf hear—all for your glory!

Sweet Holy Spirit, fill every minister beyond their capacity to imagine! May the Glory of the Lord find its resting place upon the tablets of their hearts, and cause change to occur within. Use their vessels to perform signs and wonders, and let the greatest miracle of all occur—the acceptance of salvation, the lost found, and filled with the blessed Holy Spirit!

And when their assignment has been completed, O', God, restore to strength every minister used by you on this blessed day. Bless them as they continue to press their way onward doing all to be what you have called them to be. Assign prophetic prayer warriors who will stay on the wall and will not come down until their assignments have been satisfied in the spirit. Grant the needs of your blessed ministers as they align themselves with your precepts. Fill their cups to the overflow, enlarge their territories, and grant them the spirit of completion and excellence all to the glory of your great name, in the Jesus' name, amen.

By your words I can see where I'm going; they throw a beam of light on my dark path. (PSALM 109:105)

Let Go & Let God

Every way of a man is right in his own eyes, but the LORD weighs the heart. (Proverbs 21:2)

A Thought to Ponder

In 1990, I experienced a rebirth—an awakening of the spirit to the glorious presence of the Almighty God. I later converted to the Protestant religion, at which time my first encounter involved being the recipient of what I would later deem to be sound advice: "Let go and let God." At the time, I loathed the sound of it; the thought of it was inconceivable and simply preposterous! I was simply appalled that anyone would make such a statement and then address it to me as if doing me a favor! What I found even more appalling was that I had no concept of its true meaning! Who are these people, I wondered; furthermore, what type of language are they speaking? I pondered how anyone could make sense out of a phrase that was nothing more than a religious cliché! "Let go and let God," indeed!

Years later, as I stood in the hospice ward of Stella Maris, witnessing my dad begin his journey to that state which some call death and others refer to as "peaceful rest," I could sense the presence of those saints of old peering over the balcony of glory, and imagined I could hear their eternal voices reminding me to "let go and let God." At that moment, I began to understand the painstaking truth of this cliché, which had to be experienced in order to discover the true essence of its meaning, and I wept bitterly . . .

When I released Dad into the hand of God, although painfully dreadful, I felt a sudden relief from the weight of holding on. In that blessed moment, I had discovered that letting go involves the process of emptying oneself of every preconceived notion of what and/or who they believed God to be, in exchange for fully accepting his divine providential order and purpose. It is the "laying down" of one's will for God's eternal plan, which, in the end, ushers us into the ecstasy of God's glorious abiding presence.

I ask you, is life at all what you had expected? Have you discovered the limitations of your own self-sufficiency? My advice to you is to "Let Go and Let God;" let Him teach you how to dance to the symphonic melodies of life, and move to the rhythms of Love's laughter! Only then, will you be free – indeed!

Prayer:

Eternal Father, Gracious Sovereign, thank you for the abundant life; for liberty of the spirit; for teaching us how to let go of our perspectives and preconceived notions about what and who we believe you to be, and to wholly trust in you to teach us how to move within your rhythmic patterns; to flow in your "so" love, to bask in your divine presence and be made whole, in the name of Jesus. Amen!

Amazing Grace

John John Newton (1725–1807)
Stanza 6 anon.

Amazing Grace, how sweet the sound,
That saved a wretch like me.
I once was lost but now am found,
Was blind, but now I see.

T'was Grace that taught my heart to fear.
And Grace, my fears relieved.
How precious did that Grace appear
The hour I first believed.

Through many dangers, toils and snares
I have already come;
'Tis Grace that brought me safe thus far
and Grace will lead me home.

The Lord has promised good to me.
His word my hope secures.
He will my shield and portion be,
As long as life endures.

Yea, when this flesh and heart shall fail,
And mortal life shall cease,
I shall possess within the veil,
A life of joy and peace.

When we've been here ten thousand years
Bright shining as the sun.
We've no less days to sing God's praise
Than when we've first begun.

Amazing Grace, how sweet the sound,
That saved a wretch like me.
I once was lost but now am found,
Was blind, but now I see.

"Whoever believes in me, as the Scripture has said, 'Out of his heart will flow rivers of living water.'"

(JOHN 7:38)

22

The Miracle of Salvation

Then Jesus shouted, "Father, I entrust my spirit into your hands!" And with those words he breathed his last. (Luke 23:46)

Blessed Redeemer, Mighty to Save, we marvel at the wondrous work of your salvation: the self-sacrificial yes to the Father's "so love"; how you came low to lift us high, became like us that we might be like you; died for us that we might live; shed your blessed blood to cleanse us of sin, heal us of all our diseases, and cover our nakedness! In your resurrection, we are made right with the Father.

And now, we come—with no veil between us, we come! To make our abode, we come! In humbled submission, holy adoration, exuberant praise, clothed in your robe of righteousness, free of guilt and shame and baptized in your blessed name; filled with your precious Holy Spirit, we come! Holding up that bloodstained banner as witnesses of your glorious acts, we come!

How sweet and marvelous is the wondrous work of your salvation.

May we become what we have believed . . . this day! We seal this prayer in the name of Jesus. Amen.

Holy Sovereign, Eternal God, whose presence fills immensity, wisdom without measure, intensity of love—blissful, faithfulness—always; we give you praise for allowing us to draw near and drink from the fount that never runs dry. May we drink till our heart is content and our mind renewed and transformed bearing witness to the integrity of the soul and the spirit.

Sweet Holy Spirit, God's Refining Fire, consume us with your eternal flame of love; give us to drink until we can drink no more; fill us, mold and shape us until we resemble the character of Christ Jesus in our being with every move that we make, breath breathed, thoughts, and deeds on this blessed day!

Lord of Host, by faith, we know that you will, we know that you shall, and we know that you are able to do anything but fail, in the prevailing name of Jesus. Amen.

"If anyone thirsts, let him come to me and drink. Whoever believes in me, as the Scripture has said, 'Out of his heart will flow rivers of living water.'"
(JOHN 7:37(b), 38)

O' God of Grace

See, I have appointed you this day over the nations and over the kingdoms, to pluck up and to break down, to destroy and to overthrow, to build and to plant. (Jeremiah 1:10)

Gracious Father, Lover to the Utmost, thank you for calling us to life more abundantly in you this day, for a mind to think and reason, for eyes to see your divine will, for limbs to do your good pleasure in the earth, and for a voice to give verbal testimony of your goodness on this blessed day!

King of Glory, release a divine revelation of your Supreme Majesty; shake the earth until she releases the captives into your mighty hands; grant your people holy boldness to be representatives of Jesus Christ in the earth; let your Word run swiftly throughout, overturn the charioteers and their riders; shut the mouths of the hounds of hell; bring down everything that exalt itself above your mighty name, breaking all barriers that stand between you and your beloved creation for your namesake on this blessed day!

Savior Divine, grant us the ability to walk in truth, love, and peace; may we bring glory to your name with every beat of our heart, breath, thought, action, and deed. Grant us supernatural ability to do and say only those things that are pleasing to your sight, to be aware of the dangers of an unbridled tongue, to encourage, to give with an open heart, to love to the utmost—self-emptying, self-giving, self-sacrificing . . . all to your Glory on this blessed day.

O', God of Grace, thank you for your steadfast love that never ceases, for your vigilant watch throughout the night, and the tender mercies that greet us with each new morn. Teach us to number our days, to live the abundant life, and to openly embrace your gift wholeheartedly with an opened and surrendered heart, and to render a selfless yes to your divine providential order and purpose for our lives . . . for this is the (more) abundant life—lived out in full purpose and meaning.

Sweet Holy Spirit, lead us to the fount that never runs dry; fill our cups to the overflow; saturate our being with the love of God and set our faces like a flint, transfixed to Jesus, and may we be his ambassadors in the earth—living representatives of his truth and glory.

Merciful Father, we give thanks for those who have given themselves to fasting and prayer on behalf of families everywhere, those who seek your face for revival in our land and renewal of spirit. May they be transformed in character, renewed in spirit, strengthened in body, see with clarity, and hear with correct frequency as they surrender their all to the cause of effective and fervent prayer, in Jesus's name, amen

" *W*ait for the *LORD*; be strong and
take heart and wait for the *LORD*"
(PSALMS 27:14)

Righteous Lover – Almighty God

In that day there shall be a fountain opened. (Zechariah 13:1)

Who is like God in all the earth? By the word of your power, you have set the sun, moon, and stars in their places; the seasons are on course according to divine systems and protocols, and with your breath, you alone have given life! Teach us how to number our days, how to worship you in spirit and in truth, and grant to us the ability to love you, to live according to your divine precepts, to walk before you blamelessly, to love people, and be good stewards over your creation.

Lord, Giver of every good and perfect gift, thank you for the Holy Spirit—sweet heavenly dove, your refining fire. We invite his presence into our habitation, to lead, guide, convict, and to convince; to mold and to shape our thoughts, activities, and deeds. Walk with us, and speak ever so sweetly to us on this day. May we yield not to temptation but be overcome by the love of Jesus—King of Glory, the Forgiver of our sins, Prince of Peace, that endless fount of eternal joy!

Lord of Light, Bishop and Lover of our souls, dispatch your angelic host around about us, protect our families today, guide us to open doors leading to success (in the Holy Spirit), and close doors leading to failure. Use our vessels as instruments of your peace; may a kind word bring healing and comfort to those in need.

We declare on this day that we can do all things through Jesus Christ, who is our Redeemer, the Strength of our Salvation, and soon-coming King. Grant unto us a fresh outpouring of your Holy Spirit; fill our cups today for the journey ahead; grant us divine innovation, creative genius to bless and assist those in need.

May we demonstrate loyalty and love for you through our thoughts, actions, and deeds, and may we be pleasing in your sight, in the prevailing name of Jesus. Amen!

*"For to the snow He says, 'Fall
on the earth, and to the downpour
and the rain, 'Be strong.'*
(JOB 37:6)

Fresh Fallen Snow

Let everything that has breath, praise the Lord. Praise the Lord. (Psalm 150:6)

A Thought to Ponder

When I looked out my window this morning and saw fresh snow that had fallen throughout the night, my first impression was one of complete dread! I loathed the sight of it! I could only think of the inconvenience of it all; when suddenly, that sweet and gentle still-small voice of the Holy Spirit captured my attention, and his blessed words filled my heart with deep contrition as he reminded me of the beauty of freshly fallen snow. Instantly, my perspective was transformed, and a psalm of praise broke through my heart!

"A Psalm of Praise"

Praise waits with bated breath for you! In the symphonic melodies of nature's being, from the rising of the sun until the going down of the same, praise waits with bated breath for you! In the breaking of a new morn, the cool breeze that refreshes us, in the sweet gentleness of freshly fallen snow, praise waits with bated breath for you! A new day has broken through and times of barrenness have ceased, a new horizon has risen and the freshness of a new beginning/new era/new season has suddenly smiled upon us, Praise waits with bated breath for you! And the sound of it fills each beat of our hearts with ardent praise and deep adoration; the feel of it heightens our spiritual senses to the movement of your divine presence! O', God, praise waits with bated breath for you! This is the day that the Lord has made, let us rejoice and be glad in it!

Prayer:

Gracious Father, Blessed Redeemer, thank you, for being ever so mindful of us . . . in the blessed name of Jesus. Amen!

God called the dry ground "land," and the gathered waters he called "seas."
And God saw that it was good. (Genesis 1:10)

Winter's Blast & God's Provisions

Jesus said, "Love the Lord your God with all your passion and prayer and intelligence. This is the most important, the first on any list. But there is a second to set alongside it: 'Love others as well as you love yourself.' These two commands are pegs; everything in God's Law and the Prophets hangs from them." (Matthews 22:37–40))

Lord Jesus—Mighty God, Wonderful Savior—we thank you for this winter's day, for the snow that gently falls to the ground, for the fresh air and cool breeze, for giving us time to reflect upon your tender mercies and abiding presence on this blessed day.

O', God, we pray for every state that is affected by this burst of wintry blast, for the medical teams that are working with diligence on emergency cases around the clock, for the city workers who have been busy since last Friday. Grant them all new strength, sound mind, and the tenacity to endure the storm for the sake of others. Surround them with your loving kindness, teach them to turn their faces in prayer and supplications to the one, true, and living God, and may you hear and answer their cries . . . on this blessed day.

Sweet Holy Spirit, I pray for a supernatural release of acts of extreme kindness throughout our communities, cities, and states, and for supernatural love for neighbor on this blessed day.

Precious Friend and Lover (Holy Spirit), I pray for pastors everywhere, with special intentions for Harold Alfonso Carter and Harold Alfonso Carter Jr. and family. O', God, these are men of honor, your mighty men of valor, watchmen on the wall, and men after your own heart!

We pray for their continued safety, for the neighbor who is mindful of them, and for every soul that extends a helping hand to assist them during this wintry season. Thank you for your covering over them and their families, for granting them physical and emotional stability, for visitations in the night, angelic undertakings, divine revelations, and creative power.

Lord God Almighty, we have so much to be thankful for. You have kept us from seen and unseen danger during this snowy season, kept a roof over our head, a warm bed to sleep comfortably, food, money, clothing for our bodies, and heat to keep us warm; even for the decreased focus of crime in our city, where everyone is coming together for the good of the other. We are mindful that you are our Provider, so faithful and true, whose presence is with us always—you are our god who is mighty to save. Thank you for being so gracious to our elderly during this wintry storm, for keeping our babies safe and for making a way to rescue those who are in need of extreme emergent care. Bless our firemen and Ambulatory Care Services—keep them safe as they place their lives in harm's way to take care of your people. We seal this prayer in the name of Jesus. Amen.

Yet he has not left himself without testimony: He has shown kindness by giving you rain from heaven and crops in their seasons; he provides you with plenty of food and fills your hearts with joy."

(ACTS 14:17)

Beautiful Savior – Wonderful God

He touched their eyes and said, "Become what you believe."
It happened. They saw. (Matthew 9:29)

Gracious and Merciful Father thank you for this glorious day and for every opportunity it presents to demonstrate the love of Jesus. Lord, we pray for special blessings upon those persons who demonstrate compassion and neighborly love to assist others with a true and loving heart while snowbound.

Father, thank you for unity of the spirit, the coming together of focus, intent, and effort to assist the elderly, the sick and shut-in, the widower and widow, those who would otherwise have to depend on the mercy of the city to assist them during this time of need.

God of all, thank you for those men and women who were self-sacrificial in their efforts to clean our main streets, who placed duty before pleasure and continued in their pursuit to work diligently on opening side streets. You have been so wonderful in the way you move hearts to assist those businesses and residents who are snowbound, and some even without electricity.

Sweet Holy Spirit, we feel your presence this morning in the loving concerns of our neighbors.

We pray that you would calm the fears and concerns relating to the upcoming forecast, replace fear with faith, and concerns with confidence in your abiding presence.

Lord Jesus, Wonderful Savior, we thank you for your blessed blood that heals us of all our diseases, cleanses us through and through, and covers our nakedness. We plead your blood over this United States of America, over our sons and daughters, over the unborn; the elderly, your Church Universal, over those men and women who are making special sacrifices to clear our roads for travel during this storm, over the health-care industry, our military soldiers who risk their lives for our liberty, and over the sacred covenant of marriages, and the men and women who lead our country.

Thank you for demonstrating abundance in mercy, consistency in faithfulness, and steadfastness of love. Be with us now; grant us your peace that surpasses all understanding, stability for the storms that await us, and faith in you to sustain us.

In Jesus's name. Amen.

"*He wraps up the waters in His clouds,
and the cloud does not burst under them.*

(JOB 26:8)

To Dance with God

Enoch walked with God; then he was no more, because God took him away. (Genesis 5:24)

Eternal God our Father, thank you for calling us to a brand-new morn; for giving us a mind to think and a heart to sing forth your praises; for articulation of speech; a portion of health and strength; a measure of faith; for love, joy, and peace in the Holy Spirit; and for the victory that we have in Christ Jesus, through his blessed blood that saves to the uttermost! We rise with the song of praise upon our lips and heartfelt thanksgiving, which gives testimony to the fact that this is, indeed, the day that the Lord has made and it is marvelous in our sight!

Sweet Holy Spirit, Breath of God, we give ourselves to you wholly, without hesitation or doubt, but freely do we open our heart and mind to you. Have your way—break, melt, mold, shape, and make us until we mirror the character and nature of Jesus in our being. To be like him in mind and heart, to mirror his actions and deeds, to be willing to step beyond the barriers of ignorance to embrace your way of moving. Sensitize us to your expressions and impressions.

Awaken our spiritual senses to your movement and then synchronize us to the syncopated patterns of the orchestrated choreographic movement of God that we might dance with our God—to move when he moves—in mind, heart, action, and deed! For this is the abundant life; the more excellent way to walk in syncopated rhythm with our God and Father of the Lord Jesus Christ!

O', God, hear the earnest desire of our hearts, and do all according to your divine providential order and purpose . . . in the prevailing name Jesus Christ and soon-coming King . . . Amen..

"*After this, the word of the LORD came to Abram in a vision: "Do not be afraid, Abram. I am your shield, your very great reward."*

(GENESIS 15:1)

How Great Is Our God!

"From the rising of the sun, to the place where it sets the Name of the Lord is to be praised." (Psalm 113:3)

A Thought to Ponder

Yesterday evening, I was reminded that the same glory that caused the sun to rise in the east causes it to set in the west. As I drove homeward-bound down Loch Raven Boulevard, the angelic host of heaven prompted my attention above the natural cares of the day to "see" heaven-bound events taking place in my midst. In the suddenness of that precious moment, I saw the miracle of a sunset and imagined that I could hear the voices of heaven's choir singing exhortations to our God, to wit, my spirit exclaimed, "How great is God!"

Oftentimes, the vicissitudes of life cloud our vision and cause us to miss out on God's reflective glory, even in a sunset. I was reminded of Psalm 24:1–2, to wit, "The earth is the LORD's, and the fullness thereof; the world, and they that dwell therein; For HE hath founded it upon the seas, and established it upon the floods."

God is just as great at the closing of a day/life and/or season, just as he is at the beginning. Be amazed by his wonder! Be amazed by his grace! And praise his wonderful name!

Prayer:

Gracious Father, Holy Sovereign, we are captivated by the marvelous works of your hands, the reflection of your splendor in the heavens above, and the miraculous wonders found at the ending of a day. Sensitize our spirit to your impressions so that our souls might be replenished throughout the day. May we be amazed/astound/astonished, thrilled, and captivated by the way you woo our hearts and fill us with your love. Thank you, Lord, for being mindful of us and for granting us a glimpse of your unceasing pursuit for our love and attention.

In the name of Jesus. Amen!

The Lord is exalted over all the nations, his glory above the heavens. (Psalm 113:4)

Majestic & Holy Sovereign

O' Lord, our Lord, how excellent is your name in all the earth! You have set your glory above the heavens. (Psalm 8:1)

Clothed in righteousness and supreme majesty, we tremble in your divine presence and marvel at the splendor of your glory! Our heart's cry is "Holy, Holy, Holy" in conviction of our imperfections, but convinced by the saving power of the blood of Jesus that we are indeed sanctified and made righteous as we stand in your presence divine.

Abba, you told us that in the day we call on you that you would hear, answer, and show us great and mighty things that are inconceivable for the human mind to reason.

Papa, we need your divine intervention in this world! Overturn the horses and charioteers of the enemy. Obliterate the fiery darts of deception; destroy every plot, ploy, and evil intent devised as a plan to sow the spirit of depression, oppression, and poverty. In the name of Jesus, we ask that you pull down strongholds in government and political systems everywhere; transform the minds and hearts of legislators and establish your divine government in the earthly realm; call forth lovers of God; anoint and appoint them to serve in strategic positions of power and influence, granting unto them supernatural ability and divine ideas.

Plant them in their high places; give them the Holy Ghost unction and divine stability to stand firm to the convictions of their faith in the terrible times of testing.

We come in earnest expectation knowing that you will hear and respond to our prayers according to your divine providential purpose and order. Therefore, we ask these things of a great god who is well able to perform. And we seal this prayer in the blessed name of Jesus. Amen.

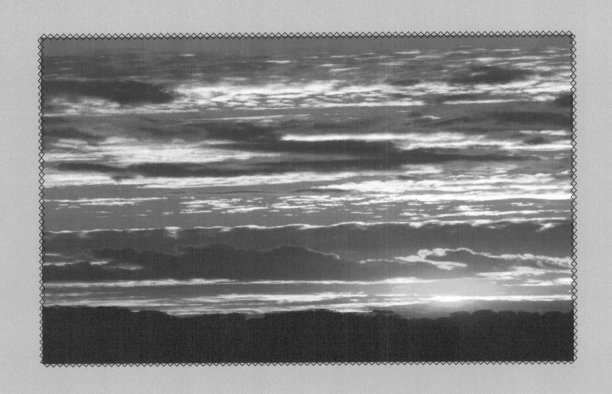

"When Jesus had received the sour wine, he said, "It is finished," and he bowed his head and gave up his spirit."

JOHN 19:30

Sovereign Ruler

O', God, you are my God, earnestly I seek you; my soul thirsts for you, my body longs for you, in a dry and weary land where there is no water. (Psalm 63:1)

Creator and Sustainer of all life, thank you for this day; for the slight breeze in the dawning of a new morn; for the dew and the birds that sing your praises ever so sweetly; for the activity of our limbs, a reasonable portion of health and strength; for a mind to reason, the articulation of speech, and for life more abundantly. We give your name the honor with a whole heart and exuberant praise; fully yours, everything within, we praise your righteous name on this day!

King of Glory, Lord of Hosts, the whole earth trembles before your mighty presence! Who can stand before you and declare they are sinless? Our nation, as a whole, have left from honoring and serving you and have turned to sin and abomination, which have contaminated our government, nation, and even our high places of worship.

Gracious Father, Forgiver of Sins, on behalf of this nation, we ask that you would forgive us for our rebellion and disobedience. Forgive us for permitting and even endorsing abominations in our land, which you despise and hate. Forgive us for abandoning you as our first love and for going after other gods.

Turn your face toward us and smile upon us; deliver us from evil and set our feet high upon the Rock; restore love, honesty, truth, godliness, justice, and righteousness in our land.

Righteous Lover, we humble ourselves before you and pray for healing in our land. Bring economic and social resolve, deliverance from lawlessness, reconciliation of families, and for souls to be saved. Thus, we repent wholeheartedly, fully conscious of your power to perform on this blessed day in Jesus's name. Amen.

But whoever drinks the water I give him will never thirst. Indeed, the water I give him will become in him a spring of water welling up to eternal life. "

(JOHN 4:14)

Supreme Lover

Take my yoke upon you and learn from me, for I am gentle and humble in heart, and you wil find rest for your souls. (Matthew 11:29)

All-Searching, Ever-Present God, you know our thoughts from afar off and read the heart, view principles, and motives of actions; and yet you—whose presences fills us immensely—bid us to come and to drink from the fount that will never run dry! And for this we are eternally grateful.

O', Holy Spirit, be our comforter, light, guide, and sanctifier. Take the things of Christ Jesus and show them to our soul; may we learn from you more of love, grace, compassion, faithfulness, and the beauty of obedience. Gracious God, come as power to reign supremely in us; come as teacher to lead us into all truth, filling us with understanding; come as love that we may have increased adoration for the Father, loving him with our whole being; come as light, illuminating our soul with your truth; come as sanctifier—body, soul, and spirit to be wholly yours; come as beautifier, bringing order out of confusion, loveliness out of chaos just as in the beginning. Do it again, even now. All-Consuming Fire of God, refine our souls for service without hesitation, without rebellion, without fear . . .

O', Merciful Father, hear our prayers! Lead us to the cross, and grant us eyes to see and a heart to receive the self-giving love of Jesus. Show us the wounds: the nails that transfixed him, the cords that bound him, the thorns that tore open his flesh, and the sword that pierced his side. Reveal to us the marvelous wonders of his statement "It is finished."

God of All, we thank you for the revelation of your glory in the face of Jesus. May we look only to Jesus, and may the glory that we see in following him closely be reflected in us so that we may look like him in all our thoughts, actions, and deeds. May all be absolved of sin and convinced that they have encountered true love through our interactions on this blessed day that the Lord has made.

Supreme Lover and Bishop of our souls, grant us the grace and mercy to love you and love people. We pray this prayer in the prevailing name that is above all names—Jesus Christ our Lord and Savior. Amen.

*"Let the same mind be in you
that was in Christ Jesus . . ."*

(Philippians 2:5-a)

God's Reflective Glory

Whatever you do, work at it with all your heart, as working for the Lord, not for men, since you know that you will receive an inheritance from the Lord as a reward. (Colossians 3:23–24)

A Thought to Ponder

In times past, I would dread the thought of Monday. Just when I was about to kick off my heels and settle down into the weekend, Monday was ever present, casting gloomy shadows of remembrance that the long-awaited weekend would soon be over!

The Holy Spirit gently delivered me from this type of thinking by reminding me that each day is a precious gift from God, and whatever I decided to do with his precious gift would make all the difference in this world. He gently encouraged me to worship God by using what God gives freely to create and develop ways that will assist those in need.

Prayer:

Holy Sovereign, Giver of every good and perfect gift, we rise to the simplicity of a new day to worship and glorify your magnificent name! Lord, grant to us divine ideas, creative ability, and innovative power in the marketplace to use what you have freely given us to provide aide and assistance to those in need. May we execute, produce, and deliver all with the Spirit of excellence, love, and great humility; and may your wonderful name be praised and glorified through the works of our hands and the demonstration of your love on this blessed day! Amen!

And they were calling to one another: "Holy, holy, holy is the LORD Almighty; the whole earth is full of his glory." (Isaiah 6:3)

The Holy Spirit came to my aide after the breaking began. He opened my eyes to the reality that there were others living around me whose sufferings were much greater than mine. He began to use me as an instrument to pray for others, and to continue to flow in ministry out of the place where the pain was the greatest. I found the strength and will to live through sorrow's valley. While my soul began to take on a new posture, suddenly, prayer took on a brand-new meaning, which ultimately transformed my perspective and approach to prayer. I began to move with God—seeing beyond human capacity and responding to life beyond my natural emotions.

During the last two years of Daddy's life in this world, I literally danced with God. There is no other way to describe how I made it through such a devastating period. I moved to the syncopated patterns of the orchestrated choreographic movement of God. We were synchronized as one. But understand there was a process that had to lead me to that place where the eternal God is.

I, therefore, contend that prayer is the bending of the will to incline one's ear to hear the heartbeat of God. It is the nevertheless in Jesus' prayer to the Father in the Garden of Gethsemane (Luke 22:39–46) and Mary's self-sacrificial yes to the Father's will above her own (Luke 1:38); it is Esther's "If I perish, I perish" (Esther 4:16), and John's famous response to his disciples, "He must increase and I must decrease" (John 3:30). When we get into a posture/position in our prayer life where we are able to hear clearly the Father's will above our own, only then do we become free indeed from the entanglement of self and begin to see further than our personal situation and circumstances, and move freely into the place of service to others.

Regrettably, it has taken over twenty years of Christian experience for me to learn that prayer is indeed the "bending of the will to incline one's ear to hear the heartbeat of God." You might ask, just how does one learn such a lesson? There are times when God will allow the vicissitudes of life (unexpected bumps in the road) to jolt us to the spiritual reality that he is so much more than what we perceive him to be, and he is with us always (Matthew 28:20b). Oftentimes, it is our perception about God that causes us to miss his glorious presence when we go to him in prayer. But then God is long-suffering and gracious, abundant in all goodness and all truth; his mercies are mysteriously new, and he will wait until the circumstances of life awaken us to the reality that his ways are indeed good for us. The prophet Isaiah was correct when he said, "As the heavens are higher than the earth, so are my ways higher than your ways and my thoughts than your thoughts" (Isaiah 55:9). When the inconceivable is made known by way of divine revelation, all our defenses slowly dissipate into nothingness; and suddenly, with a bowed-down head, the very core of which we are surrenders to the glorious revelation of God's abiding presence, and exclaim, to wit, "God is great!"

The true moment of prayer's resolve is God's abiding presence discovered in our circumstances. It is in that sacred place of abiding that we encounter the presence of God and realize that for whatever reason we hastened to his throne, it could never exceed the fullness of joy found in his divine presence. In that sacred place, we learn how to release our burdens in exchange for the encounter: to hear God's voice (which is fulfilling in itself) directing, leading, and teaching us a more excellent way to be and experience life

Such a discovery activates the spiritual senses and allows us to see for the very first time that God's purpose for our lives encompasses the world around us! When we discover and accept God's will above our own, only then shall we truly rise from our beds of affliction, just as Peter's mother rose from her sickbed to give service (Matthew 8:14–15); we shall rise from our slumber, just as Jarius's dead daughter rose to the voice of the Master (Mark 5:35–43); we shall rise to a new life with new vigor, just as the Lord Jesus Christ rose from the dead with all power in his hand! So shall we rise above our circumstances and rest in God's divine will for our lives. He is faithful and well able to bring to completion that good work that he has begun in us (**Philippians 1:6**).

Truly, I tell you, when we have understood what prayer is, we would have discovered prayer's resolve. Establish your own connectedness with God in prayer by bending your will to the will of the Father. Only then will you recognize his voice above your own and learn how to dance to the rhythm within.

PRAYER:

Lord God, we thank you for the depth of your love toward us and for being the cause of our strength and ability to walk through sorrow's valley. Thank you for hearing our prayers and for your response to our requests. Fill our hearts with joy, and cause your laughter to fill our souls with a new and vibrant hope in your ability to do the impossible in and through us for your glorious namesake, the Lord Jesus Christ. Amen.

He said to me: "It is done. I am the Alpha and the Omega, the Beginning and the End. To him who is thirsty I will give to drink without cost from the spring of the water of life." (Revelation 21:6)

As The Deer (Song)

As the deer panteth for the water
So my soul longeth after Thee
You alone are my heart's desire
And I long to worship Thee

Chorus:
You alone are my strength, my shield
To You alone may my spirit yield
You alone are my heart's desire
And I long to worship Thee

You're my friend and You are my brother
Even though You are a king
I love You more than any other
So much more than anything

(Chorus)

I want You more than gold or silver
Only You can satisfy
You alone are the real joy giver
And the apple of my eye

by Martin Nystrom 1984